Your notes and drawings ↑↑↑

Your notes and drawings ↑↑↑

Your notes and drawings ↑↑↑

Your notes and drawings ↑↑↑

Your notes and drawings ↑↑↑

Your notes and drawings ↑↑↑

Your notes and drawings ↑↑↑

Your notes and drawings ↑↑↑

Your notes and drawings ↑↑↑

Your notes and drawings ↑↑↑

Your notes and drawings ↑↑↑

Your notes and drawings ↑↑↑

Your notes and drawings ↑↑↑

Your notes and drawings ↑↑↑

Your notes and drawings ↑↑↑

Your notes and drawings ↑↑↑

Your notes and drawings ↑↑↑

Your notes and drawings ↑↑↑

Your notes and drawings ↑↑↑

Your notes and drawings ↑↑↑

Your notes and drawings ↑↑↑

Your notes and drawings ↑↑↑

Your notes and drawings ↑↑↑

Your notes and drawings ↑↑↑

Your notes and drawings ↑↑↑

Your notes and drawings ↑↑↑

Your notes and drawings ↑↑↑

Your notes and drawings ↑↑↑

Your notes and drawings ↑↑↑

Your notes and drawings ↑↑↑

Your notes and drawings ↑↑↑

Your notes and drawings ↑↑↑

Your notes and drawings ↑↑↑

Your notes and drawings ↑↑↑

Your notes and drawings ↑↑↑

Your notes and drawings ↑↑↑

Your notes and drawings ↑↑↑

Your notes and drawings ↑↑↑

Your notes and drawings ↑↑↑

Your notes and drawings ↑↑↑

Your notes and drawings ↑↑↑

Your notes and drawings ↑↑↑

Your notes and drawings ↑↑↑

Your notes and drawings ↑↑↑

Your notes and drawings ↑↑↑

Your notes and drawings ↑↑↑

Your notes and drawings ↑↑↑

Your notes and drawings ↑↑↑

Your notes and drawings ↑↑↑

Your notes and drawings ↑↑↑

Your notes and drawings ↑↑↑

Your notes and drawings ↑↑↑

Your notes and drawings ↑↑↑

Your notes and drawings ↑↑↑

Your notes and drawings ↑↑↑

Your notes and drawings ↑↑↑

Your notes and drawings ↑↑↑

Your notes and drawings ↑↑↑

Your notes and drawings ↑↑↑

Your notes and drawings ↑↑↑

Your notes and drawings ↑↑↑

Your notes and drawings ↑↑↑

Your notes and drawings ↑↑↑

Your notes and drawings ↑↑↑

Your notes and drawings ↑↑↑

Your notes and drawings ↑↑↑

Your notes and drawings ↑↑↑

Your notes and drawings ↑↑↑

Your notes and drawings ↑↑↑

Your notes and drawings ↑↑↑

Your notes and drawings ↑↑↑

Your notes and drawings ↑↑↑

Your notes and drawings ↑↑↑

Your notes and drawings ↑↑↑

Your notes and drawings ↑↑↑

Your notes and drawings ↑↑↑

Your notes and drawings ↑↑↑

Your notes and drawings ↑↑↑

Your notes and drawings ↑↑↑

Your notes and drawings ↑↑↑

Your notes and drawings ↑↑↑

Your notes and drawings ↑↑↑

Your notes and drawings ↑↑↑

Your notes and drawings ↑↑↑

Your notes and drawings ↑↑↑

Your notes and drawings ↑↑↑

Your notes and drawings ↑↑↑

Your notes and drawings ↑↑↑

Your notes and drawings ↑↑↑

Your notes and drawings ↑↑↑

Your notes and drawings ↑↑↑

Your notes and drawings ↑↑↑

Your notes and drawings ↑↑↑

Your notes and drawings ↑↑↑

Your notes and drawings ↑↑↑

Your notes and drawings ↑↑↑

Your notes and drawings ↑↑↑

Your notes and drawings ↑↑↑

Your notes and drawings ↑↑↑

Your notes and drawings ↑↑↑

Your notes and drawings ↑↑↑

Your notes and drawings ↑↑↑

Your notes and drawings ↑↑↑

Your notes and drawings ↑↑↑

Your notes and drawings ↑↑↑